WHEN CLERGYMEN
RULED THE EARTH

To the Rev. 'Aqualung' Morgan
(who failed to hold me under
long enough during my baptism)
this book is affectionately dedicated.

WHEN CLERGYMEN RULED THE EARTH

SIMON JENKINS

MINSTREL

Eastbourne

First published 1991

Cover design by Simon Jenkins

British Library Cataloguing in Publication Data

Jenkins Simon 1954 –
When clergymen ruled the earth.
1. English cartoons. Special subjects. Christianity
I. Title
741.5942

ISBN 1-85424-081-1

Printed in Great Britain for
Minstrel, an imprint of Monarch Publications
1 St Anne's Road, Eastbourne, E Sussex BN21 3UN by
Richard Clay Ltd, Bungay, Suffolk

Introduction

In 1987, an image of the face of Christ mysteriously appeared on an ordinary window pane in Rome. The miraculous window became an immediate shrine, drawing large crowds each day to behold this new wonder. When the police were called in to control it all, they made a startling discovery: *the glass was dirty*. One wipe, and the miracle was over.

Religion is a serious business, but ironically, the more seriously people take their religion (and themselves) the funnier they can become. The Pope takes seriously his ceremony of kissing the runway tarmac at each new country he visits – but it still makes amusing television. And when the piece of tarmac is dug up and venerated (as happened when the Pope visited Britain in 1982), amusement turns to outright laughter.

One of the great strengths of Christianity is its realism about human nature, and its ability to make us laugh at our own folly. As Malcolm Muggeridge put it: 'Christianity is one of the great fosterers of humour, because it expresses more than any other religion ever has the sense of the inadequacy of men in relation to their aspirations after perfection.'

This book is an attempt to step (or fall) into the great humorous tradition of Christianity. Special thanks are due to Adrian Reith, who collaborated on the cartoon captions over a couple of tandoori suppers. And to all those who have shown me (intentionally or not) that faith and laughter do go hand in hand.

Simon Jenkins

Simon Jenkins sat through an estimated 5,000 hours of sermons, church notices, Sunday school outings and faith-sharing pot noodle suppers to produce this book. He is a graduate in theology and works in London as a freelance cartoonist, writer and editor. His previous books include a cartoon introduction to the Bible, *The Bible from Scratch*.

Teething problems with the new baptistry.

The market in owned pews had hit an all-time low.

Quality-control at the Dog Collar Works.

Rev. Ditchwater's sermons were so bad that people were known to 'fall asleep' in the biblical sense.

Eventually, the Receiver had to be called in.

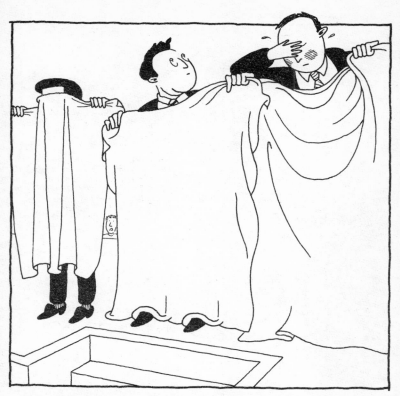

On contact with the water, Felicity's baptismal gown dissolved.

*The trouble with Rev. Morgan was that he couldn't help
taking his work home.*

The opportunity for mindless repetition was never passed up
at the Be Bold Fellowship.

Hi-tech heckling.

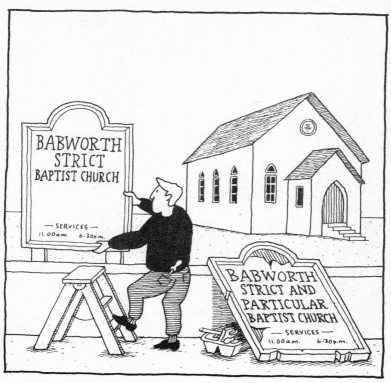

Some said it was the thin end of the wedge.

First Presbyterian shunned modern translations.

It was no use. The air bubble refused to budge.

The 20-minute grace.

'So exactly how many Hail Marys is that, Father?'

The church in an alternative universe.

Bell-ringing, Pentecostal style.

Taking up the collection at St. Rothschild's.

A record-breaking congregation was expected at Midnight Mass.

The difference between a pope and an archbishop.

The dance group's 'Tower of Babel' routine
was approaching its shattering climax.

Ecclesiastical space-walking.

The lipstick problem at the Greek Orthodox church.

The Seaman's Mission.

The staff didn't know it, but the Pizza Palace was about to become a major Catholic shrine.

The night of the Baptist communion wine wreckers.

*It was then that Desmond realised that
total immersion was not for him.*

Sunday school at the Snake-handling Pentecostal church.

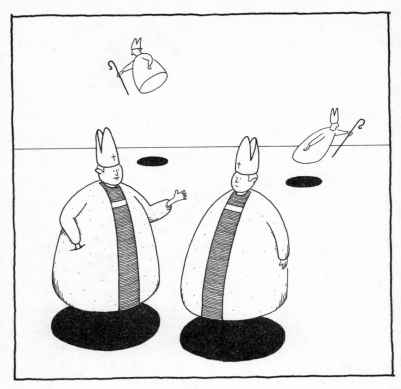

Bishops of the future.

Sometimes Rev. Pyle seemed to be in a world of his own.

Roxeter Baptist, twinned with Vyguli Baptist in Central Siberia.

Rev. 'Aqualung' Morgan's reputation went before him.

Robo-Pope.

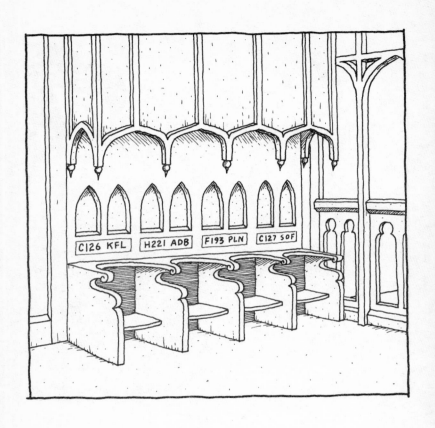

The J.W. Trap worked like a dream.

Precautions were taken against any further outbreaks of charismatic activity.

Undergoing sponsored immersion was Gilbert's particular ministry.

Chris the Calvinist just lived for pleasure.

Mrs Mogadon preferred short sermons.

There was something about the Richardsons that marked them out as readers of the Good News Bible.

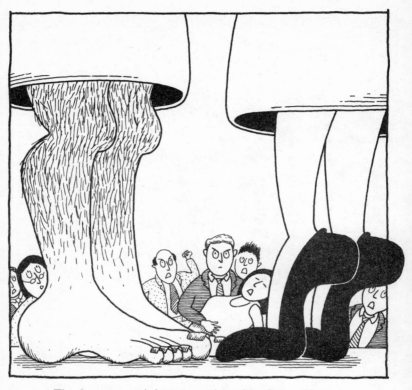

The dance group's interpretation of the Song of Songs could not be faulted on biblical accuracy.

*The new Fellowship Group Control System
was a vast improvement.*

The danger of charismatic worship in low gravity.

*The trial of the 'sit through any sermon' hat
was going better than expected.*

*Some felt that the church might have lost something
in the refurbishment.*

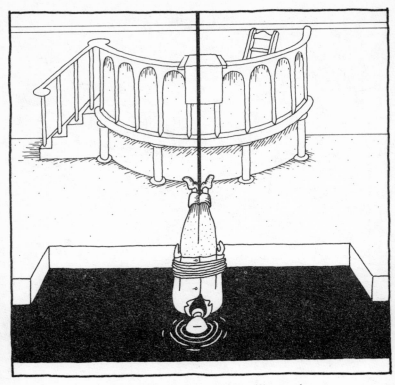

Pastor Reed was keen on sermon illustrations.

Stone Age church.

Doom Street Baptist was a home from home for the dark stranger.

*Firemen refused to wear breathing apparatus
at the Incense Factory fire.*

The 'campaign for shorter sermons' was finally beginning to get through.

Pastor Cooper was big on tithing.

*The bishop's controversial 'Go Forth and Multiply' sermon
had been about nine months before.*

Starting with the head, the first-ever attempt at an adult total immersion in three inches of water was under way.

The new curate's first sermon.

The bishop could always be sure of an old-fashioned welcome
at St Uriah's.

The TV evangelist repents.

*The visiting Hindustani scholar explained the unfortunate,
true meaning of what Deirdre had said in tongues.*

Processions were rather important to Bishop Nigel.

Rev. Smoothman fails to make a good first impression with the deacons.

The quality of students at the Walking on Water Class
had seriously declined.

The spring collection of Baptismal Wear was always popular.

'My theme for today is effective communication...'

'And now, in reverse order...'

*News that the word 'tithe' meant 'one-quarter' rather than
'one-tenth' was not warmly received.*

Things were never quite the same after women's ordination.

With hindsight, Mr Arnold really should have switched off his radio mike before leaving the platform.

The priest who wore a lounge suit to his own ordination.

Even a single dry patch would invalidate the baptism.

*In an act of calculated cruelty, he included a hymn
too high for the choir to sing…*

After the off, no further bets were allowed.

The Methodist mole's cover was well and truly blown.

Rev. Ogmore-Pritchard carefully explained what Paul meant when he said, 'Use a little wine for thy stomach's sake'.

The deacons choose the material for the new female baptismal gowns.

'Would sir prefer it with or without sequins?'

*No one could accuse the Abbey of measuring success
in crude numerical terms.*

Second thoughts about the new organist.

The leap of faith.

Appointing Mr Wildbore as organist had been a bit of a gamble.

It was then that the bishop's guilty secret came out.

Bethesda was the proud holder of the deepest baptistry record.

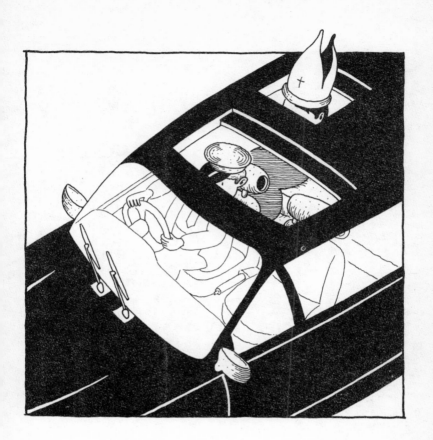

Rapture practice.

*Norman won the Wet Cassock Competition
for the third year in succession.*

Rev. Manly couldn't get out of the habit.

The vicar firmly refuted the 'valium-in-the-communion-wine'
accusation as gutter press sensationalism.

Women had a definite place in the Springs in the Desert Restoration Fellowship.

Gerald had never been entirely convinced by the famous
'weeping Calvin' of Geneva.

What train-spotters do on Sunday.

St Peugeot's midnight motor-masses were a huge success.

*The invention of the periscope was revolutionising worship
at St Matilda's.*

The concept of church discipline was foreign to some new converts.

Pastor Wilson's excommunication technique owed something to his career in the Air Force.

Baptism school.

*His first thought was that the rapture had just ruined
a perfectly good church roof.*